Fine as San Diego

GREG LAWSON

Oakana House

Fine as San Diego

Photography by

GREG LAWSON

ISBN 978-0-9762197-0-5

Printed and bound in Korea by Sung-In Printing Co., Ltd.

WWW.GregLawsonGalleries.com

Lawson logo is a registered trademark of Greg Lawson

Cover and pages 2 & 3: Sandstone meets surf at Sunset Cliffs Park

Title page: San Diego Bay and city skyline

Serra Museum in Old Town San Diego's Presidio Park

San Diego Purple Coral is acquired from the depths off San Clemente Island

"*America's Finest City.*" It seems no matter where I go in the world, San Diego, as its motto denotes, is known and cherished as one of the USA's favored destinations. What makes it such? Of course there are many answers, but if pressed to select just one, many would quickly respond "*The weather!*"

The Southern California coastal strip from Point Conception southward arguably offers the most equable weather in the continental forty-eight states. When measured by this standard, the finest of the fine will surely prove to be along the San Diego share.

However it is not that consistency, but rather a grand diversity, reflected in the natural elements, that defines the region's superiority for many of us. Topographic features of the landscape help organize patterns of positive or negative oceanic influence and in turn create a sweeping range of climatic variation on a very small map. Assume a fixed position somewhere in the greater San Diego heartland, then gravitate in any single direction for less than an hour by car and you will have traversed and experienced provincial distinctions and mergers of conspicuous dimension.

Agriculturally the area provides a quick read of that varietal scope as well. In a relatively short span one can meander from flower and strawberry fields, to citrus and avocado groves, upward through vineyards to pine and spruce elevations which are aptly suited for apple and pear production. Quickly then, you'll descend to the intensity of true desert conditions where heat demanding citrus and dates can thrive in their own nurturing environment.

On the social side, our network of cities and towns has many distinguished neighborhoods now showcasing a truly multi-cultural society. There seems a particular pride in the native peoples' emergence, not merely as an economic force, but especially in their role as a pronounced and positive influence for the good of the greater community. The geographic positioning of the region naturally encourages a symbiosis with our influential neighbors, greater Los Angeles and Mexico.

The collection of images in *Fine as San Diego* purposes to celebrate nature's distinctions in this privileged pocket of Southern California. Some of the images herein will not reflect recent changes made to the landscape, either by whims of nature or by the hand of man.

I sincerely hope your experiences here will prove to be, like the region itself, as fine as San Diego!

Greg Lawson

Sandstone cave nosing into La Jolla Bay

Left: Lacy wave of the Pacific coast washes ashore near Del Mar

Coastal breezes support soaring enthusiast near the gliderport adjacent to Salk Institute

Geisel Library, on the campus of UCSD

Mixed flocks interact in a tranquil setting, Batiquitos Lagoon

Tumbled deposits at San Elijo State Beach, Cardiff-by-the-Sea

Inspiring view of La Jolla Bay, the Torreys and the heavens

Seaside box lunch delivery for beachcomber

Dusk settles on Torrey Pines Municipal Golf Course and its coastal view

California Tower rises some 200' above the landscaped gardens of Balboa Park

Mission Bay, the San Diego skyline and the view to Mexico from Soledad Mountain

A promontory view for Fort Rosecrans National Cemetery

Intriguing Dragon Tree structure, Ellen Browning Scripps Park

Hi-rise backdrop for Torrey Pines City Beach

Protected limbs of young Torrey pines safely outstretched in their reserve

Seaspray on a rocky shelf, La Jolla

Pacific breaker batters San Diego coastline

Small sandpipers and lapping tide, San Onofre State Beach

Bluff erosion along the Del Mar coast

Peaceful flow at the San Dieguito River estuary, Del Mar

Ritual gathering of cormorants, gulls and pelicans for a taste of coastal splash

Mission Beach, a pocket community between the beach and Mission Bay

Left: Mixed pleasure vessels in San Diego Bay

San Diego-Coronado Bridge, the graceful curve over San Diego Bay

Fan palm and yucca in the gardens of Balboa Park

Aerial survey of Coronado Municipal Beach

Previous: Early morning moonset at the Point as seen from Silver Strand State Beach

Nature's outcroppings are a protective seawall for La Jolla Cove

Blossom-time brightens immigrant ice plant with near neon hues

The sharp eye of a California Brown Pelican considers the maritime menu

Moment in the sun

Flush of dawn at Chula Vista Harbor

Battered shells blanket sand on South Beach, Coronado

Seal pup nursing, Ellen Browning Scripps Park

Old Point Loma lighthouse at Cabrillo National Monument

Sights, sounds and smells impose a seaside reverie

Gulls frolic in their element, Coronado Municipal Beach

Pelican trio rests before flight

Adapted botanicals on a seaside perch. La Jolla

Heaven's spotlight and historic Starvation Mountain

Del Mar demarcation of land and sea

Waning light effects a moody sea

Treasured Torrey pine is preserved and protected in its native seaside soil

The 'Star' with stars and stripes

Right: 'Star of India' ploughing Pacific waters on a rare sail

Sandstone cliffs backdrop Torrey Pines State Beach

Hotel 'Del' . . . the timeless face of Coronado

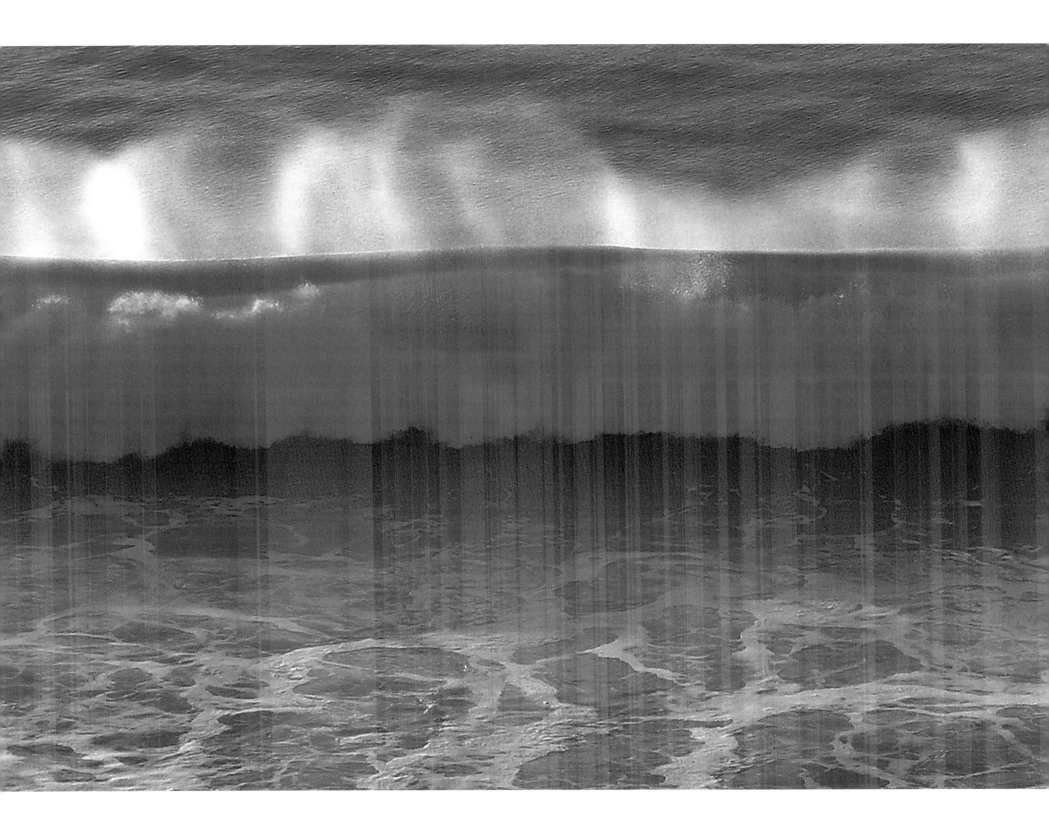

Extended wave rolls ashore at Del Mar coast

Prized architecture partly obscured by Balboa Park botanicals

Surfers and wader at La Jolla coast

Talented organist plays the Spreckels Organ

San Diego's solar power bids good night

Lake Sutherland offers a peaceful retreat for anglers and boaters

Winter's palette over San Marcos hilltops

Lizard's Tail abounds in fresh water wetlands

Historic Leucadia field of colorful ranunculus

Overnight storm gives birth to seldom seen snowfall at half-mile altitude

Winter's mantle on San Diego County's highest peak, 6533' Hot Springs Mountain

Fiery seasonal color warns of poison oak

Young bobcat peers from boulder habitat

Light breaks through rolling cloud cover in mountainous terrain near Lakeside

For San Diegans, this is the backside of Cuyamaca Peak

Vermillion is the color of Fall for pistacia planted near Oak Grove

The Lavender Fields grace country slopes with pleasant shades and pleasing scents near Valley Center

Ramona Valley and San Pasqual Valley are exclusive American Viticultural Areas of San Diego County

Element sculpted stone in the rocky hills surrounding Barona Valley

Heavy with trunk and limb, gargantuan oak varieties survive hundreds of years throughout the region

Wetter years support a floral mix of lupine, clover and poppy in the eastern foothills

Poison oak gets a stranglehold on the torso of an Engelmann oak

Lake Morena, surrounded by the Cleveland National Forest, remains a place for isolation

Plants from Africa, Australia and South America in an ideal regional merger

Impaired poplar faces storm in historic Rancho San Jose del Valle

Rouge tint of low winter sun in lofty heartlands

Citrus on the floor, blooming avocado on the slopes, San Pasqual Valley

Ceanothus' color profusion gives rise to a common name, California Lilac, here with laurel sumac

Native sumac bursts forth with bloom on the rim of Highland Valley

San Dieguito River dammed to form Lake Hodges

Native sycamore and willow show off their Fall wardrobe

Mid-summer tones of inland valley oak forest near Black Mountain

Icy blanket of white in the Laguna Mountains

Fast-paced storm portends more snowfall in the Volcans

Coast live oak wintering on the eastern edge of its comfort zone, near Warner Springs

Cloud shadows Volcan Mountains and San Felipe Valley

Rough and tumble desert transition area near Ranchita

Solar fire reflected above Mount Woodson

Early Summer fog . . .

. . . and Winter's greening of the Santa Ysabel Creek area, Cleveland National Forest

Golden glow on the north side of Rock Mountain

Massive Summer boiler dwarfs the Peninsular Range's 6500' signature

Morning light enhances an inland deception when low fog makes mountains appear as islands of the sea

Smoke and ash rise in fire season to choke every living thing

Characteristic end-of-season color on California sycamore

Combed cloud in azure sky over hilltop oaks

El Cajon Mountain is 'El Capitan' of the Peninsular Range

Graceful waterfall fills secluded Devil's Punchbowl

Lupine and pine in Laguna Mountains

Apple tree blossoms are forerunners of Julian apple pies

Strong lines of a dormant desert poplar

Peek-a-boo sunrise at Middle Peak

Sylvan blush for Engelmann oak and eucalyptus

Soft whites and greens herald a mountain Spring

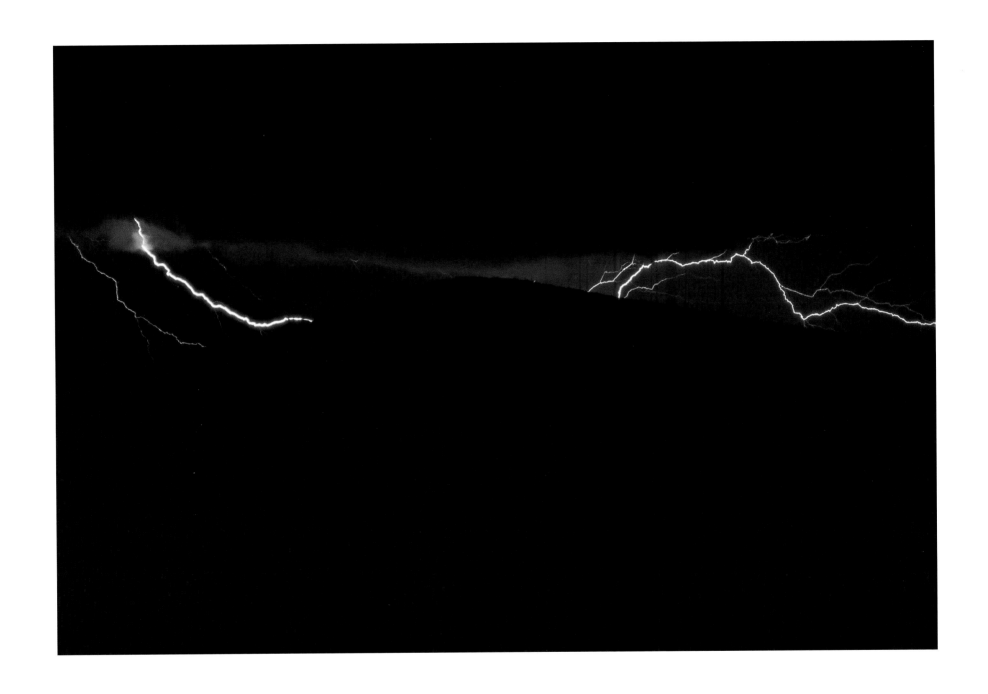

Horizontal lightning strike, Ballena

Low clouds move in to announce the conclusion to a long, dry season

Wild turkeys migrate throughout the backcountry

Cuyamaca Peak and flank of Eagle Peak

End of the rainbow, Santa Teresa Valley

118

River of rock flows near Clevenger Canyon

Soaring, searching Red-tailed Hawk

California Lilac and Engelmann oak

Cuyamaca moon

Fresh snow on Palomar Mountain as seen in the light of a silvery moon

Nature's charms in a canyon near Rancho Bernardo features pretty but pesty tamarisk

Clouds clinging to the Pacific side of the Lagunas

Scissors Crossing, a verdant desert intersection below Grapevine Mountain

Right: Field of poppies, the California state flower, above Lake Henshaw

Ocotillo and Indian Head Mountain

Left: Mortero Palms, native stand of California fan palms in an oasis setting

Brittlebush blossoms, like a million lights switched on to brighten desert slopes

Barely perceptible rosy hue downcast into a Sonoran haze

Generous blooms in Culp Valley, Anza-Borrego Desert State Park

An air of mystery in mixed desert lighting around Truckhaven Rocks

Teddy Bear cholla spines are not as innocent as the name implies

Shaggy specimens of the Seventeen Palms oasis

Chuparosa is Spanish for 'hummingbird' and its rich nectar is a desert magnet for them

Borrego Palm Canyon color following plentiful rains

Boulder trap, Anza-Borrego Desert State Park

Desert primrose on sandy slopes

Sand verbena carpets low desert

Weary vegetation yields to Summer's spell

141

Perilous placement for flower in wash, Anza-Borrego Desert State Park

1

2 / 3

5

6

8

27

28

29

30

31

32

51

52

53

54

55

56

75

76

77

78

79

80

99

100

101

102

103

104

123

124

125

126

127

128

9

10

11

12 / 13

14

33

34 / 35

36

37

38

57

58 / 59

60

61

62

81

82

83

84

85

86

105

106

107

108

109

110

129

130

131

132

133

134

15

16

17

18

19

20

39

40

41

42

43

44

63

64

65

66

67

68

87

88

89

90

91

92

111

112

113

114

115

116

135

136

137

138

139

140

GREG LAWSON JOINS WITH OAKANA HOUSE PUBLISHERS IN GRATEFULLY ACKNOWLEDGING THE WORK OF THE MANY
WHOSE CONTRIBUTIONS HAVE MADE THIS WORK POSSIBLE, INCLUDING:

Martha Barnette

Ralph Cernuda

Earl Geyer

Erick Hale

Bill Jenkin

Fortunata Lawson

Kristina Lawson

Katherine Paulos

Barry W. Smith

Darlene Smith

Don I. Suh

Person X

A tribute to the victims of the Cedar Fire

*This classic view from Banner Grade, going from verdance
to comparative barrenness will, for the time being, be just a memory*

21

22

23

24

25

26

45

46 / 47

48

49

50

69

70

71

72 / 73

74

93

94

95

96

97

98

117

118

119

120

121

122

141

142

143

144

Clockwise Gatefold Images

Full moon, San Diego Bay

Previous: Sweeney Pass area, Anza-Borrego Desert State Park

Barrel cactus' thrive in the rocky wonderland east of the Tecate Divide

Barrel cactus near Hellhole canyon